FLORIDA TEST PREP

FAST Mathematics Skills Workbook

Daily Star Practice

Kindergarten

© 2023 by Franklin Thomas

All rights reserved. No part of this book may be reproduced or transmitted in any form or by any means, electronic, mechanical, photocopying, recording, or otherwise without prior written permission.

ISBN 9798868260681

TEST MASTER PRESS

CONTENTS

Introduction	**4**
Warm-Up Practice Sets	**5**
Practice Set 1	5
Practice Set 2	9
Practice Set 3	13
Practice Set 4	17
Practice Set 5	21
Practice Set 6	25
Practice Set 7	29
Practice Set 8	33
Practice Set 9	37
Practice Set 10	41
Mini Practice Tests	**45**
Practice Set 11	45
Practice Set 12	51
Practice Set 13	57
Practice Set 14	63
Practice Set 15	69
Practice Set 16	75
Practice Set 17	81
Practice Set 18	87
Practice Set 19	93
Practice Set 20	99
Answer Key	**105**

INTRODUCTION
For Parents, Teachers, and Tutors

About the New Florida Assessment of Student Thinking (F.A.S.T.)

Students in Florida will take the Florida Assessment of Student Thinking (F.A.S.T.). This is a Progress Monitoring System that involves taking tests throughout the school year to show current level and progress. Students in Kindergarten will take the Star Mathematics test produced by Renaissance Learning. The tests are taken three times throughout the year. This book will prepare students for the Star Mathematics tests.

About Florida's New Mathematics Standards

Student learning and assessment in Florida is based on the skills listed in the new Benchmarks for Excellent Student Thinking, or B.E.S.T. The mathematics standards are divided into five broad domains, with specific benchmarks within each domain. This workbook covers every domain and benchmark.

Ongoing Skill Development and Test Practice

The Star Mathematics tests assess math skills by having students answer 34 multiple-choice questions with four answer choices. The aim of this book is to give students ongoing practice with questions like those on the Star tests. Students can complete practice sets similar to the real Star tests, but shorter.

Completing the Practice Sets

The first ten sets have 6 questions covering every domain. This allows students to become familiar with answering test questions before moving on to longer sets. These are also perfect for guided practice, and to allow review and feedback after each set.

The second ten sets have 10 questions covering every domain. Students can complete these sets independently for comprehensive test practice.

On the real tests, audio is enabled so that the questions can be read to the students. These tests can be given to students by reading each question. If students complete the sets independently, questions have been written as simply as possible to reduce reading demands.

Warm-Up

Practice Set 1

Instructions

Read each question carefully.

Each question has four answer choices.

Fill in the circle for the correct answer.

1 How many candles are there?

Ⓐ 6
Ⓑ 7
Ⓒ 8
Ⓓ 9

2 Which number is thirty-five?

Ⓐ 32
Ⓑ 33
Ⓒ 34
Ⓓ 35

3 What number is added to 4 to make 10?

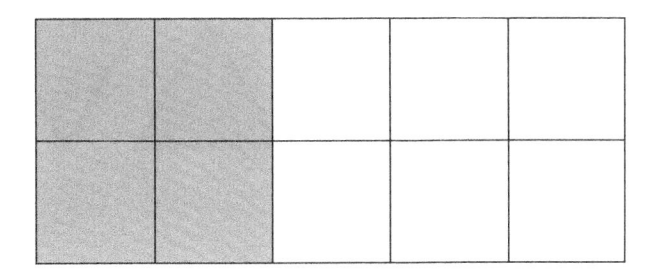

Ⓐ 4
Ⓑ 5
Ⓒ 6
Ⓓ 7

4 What is this showing about the knife?

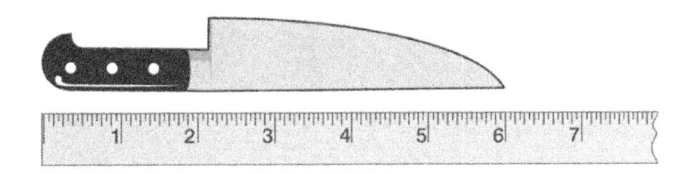

Ⓐ how heavy it is
Ⓑ how long it is
Ⓒ how old it is
Ⓓ how sharp it is

5 What two shapes are shown?

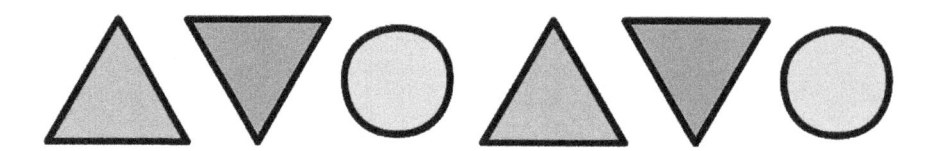

△ ▽ ○ △ ▽ ○

- Ⓐ circle and square
- Ⓑ circle and rectangle
- Ⓒ triangle and square
- Ⓓ triangle and circle

6 How many carrots are there?

- Ⓐ 5
- Ⓑ 6
- Ⓒ 7
- Ⓓ 8

Warm-Up

Practice Set 2

Instructions

Read each question carefully.

Each question has four answer choices.

Fill in the circle for the correct answer.

1 Which set has 11 camels?

Ⓐ
Ⓑ
Ⓒ
Ⓓ

2 What number is shown?

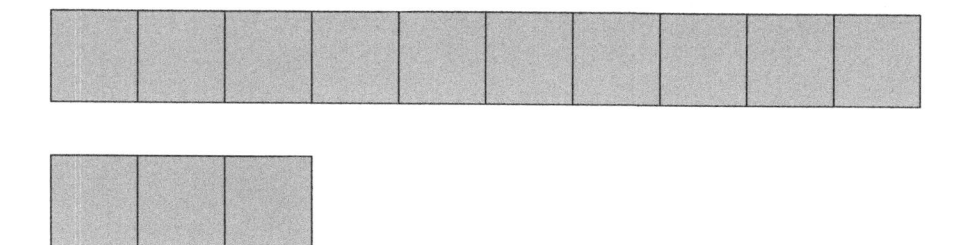

Ⓐ 1 ten + 3 ones

Ⓑ 1 ten + 13 ones

Ⓒ 10 tens + 3 ones

Ⓓ 10 tens + 13 ones

3 What is equal to 7?

Ⓐ 5 + 1

Ⓑ 5 + 2

Ⓒ 5 + 3

Ⓓ 5 + 4

4 How is the pig different from the lion?

Ⓐ heavier

Ⓑ fuller

Ⓒ shorter

Ⓓ taller

5 Which shape has the most sides?

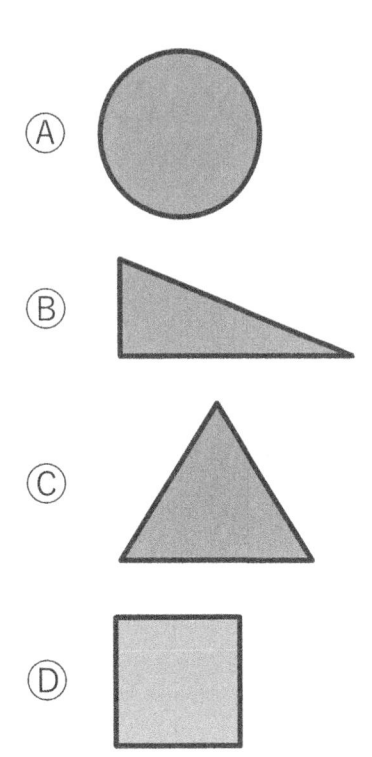

Ⓐ (circle)

Ⓑ (triangle)

Ⓒ (triangle)

Ⓓ (square)

6 Which object are there 5 of?

Ⓐ butterfly
Ⓑ ball
Ⓒ fish
Ⓓ cake

Warm-Up

Practice Set 3

Instructions

Read each question carefully.

Each question has four answer choices.

Fill in the circle for the correct answer.

1   In what place is the ball?

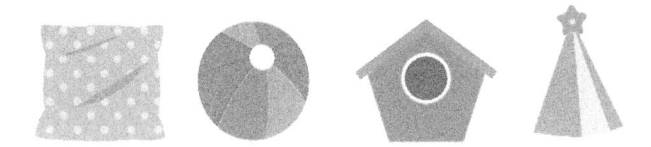

   Ⓐ   first
   Ⓑ   second
   Ⓒ   third
   Ⓓ   fourth

2   Which number goes in the box?

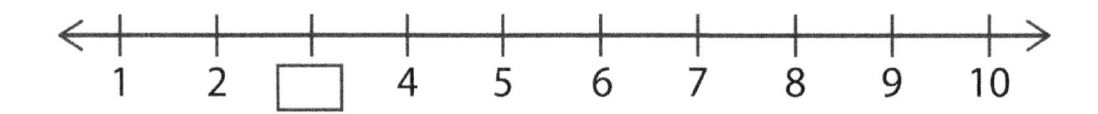

   Ⓐ   2
   Ⓑ   3
   Ⓒ   4
   Ⓓ   5

3   There are 4 bees on one plant and 5 bees on another.

How many bees are there in all?

Ⓐ   7
Ⓑ   8
Ⓒ   9
Ⓓ   10

4   How long is the saw?

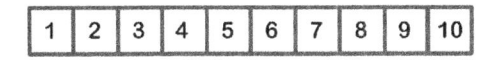

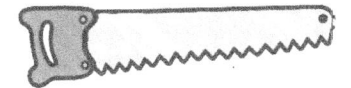

Ⓐ   5 units
Ⓑ   6 units
Ⓒ   7 units
Ⓓ   8 units

5 Which two are the same shape?

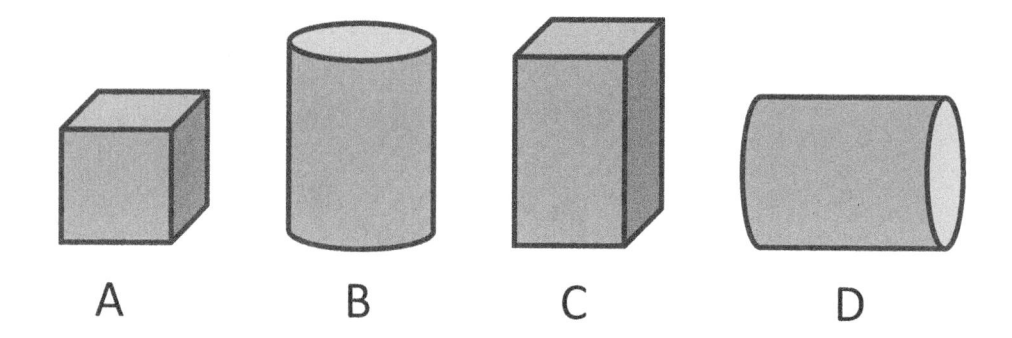

    Ⓐ A and C

    Ⓑ B and C

    Ⓒ C and D

    Ⓓ B and D

6 Which animal is there the least of?

    Ⓐ giraffe

    Ⓑ kangaroo

    Ⓒ monkey

    Ⓓ sheep

Warm-Up

Practice Set 4

> **Instructions**
>
> Read each question carefully.
>
> Each question has four answer choices.
>
> Fill in the circle for the correct answer.

1. In which set are the number of suns and clouds equal?

Ⓐ ☼ ☼ ☼ ☼ ☼ ☁ ☁ ☁

Ⓑ ☼ ☁ ☁ ☁ ☁ ☁ ☁ ☼

Ⓒ ☼ ☁ ☼ ☁ ☼ ☁ ☼ ☁

Ⓓ ☁ ☁ ☼ ☼ ☼ ☼ ☼ ☁

2. What is 10 + 7?

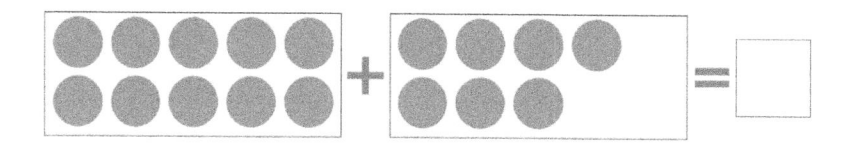

Ⓐ 3
Ⓑ 8
Ⓒ 15
Ⓓ 17

3 What does the picture show?

Ⓐ 3 + 2 = 5
Ⓑ 3 + 3 = 6
Ⓒ 3 + 4 = 7
Ⓓ 3 + 5 = 8

4 What is being found?

Ⓐ height
Ⓑ length
Ⓒ volume
Ⓓ weight

5 What shape is the frame?

Ⓐ circle
Ⓑ square
Ⓒ rectangle
Ⓓ triangle

6 Which shows how many oranges there are?

Ⓐ
Ⓑ
Ⓒ
Ⓓ

Warm-Up

Practice Set 5

Instructions

Read each question carefully.

Each question has four answer choices.

Fill in the circle for the correct answer.

1. Which set has 4 lamps?

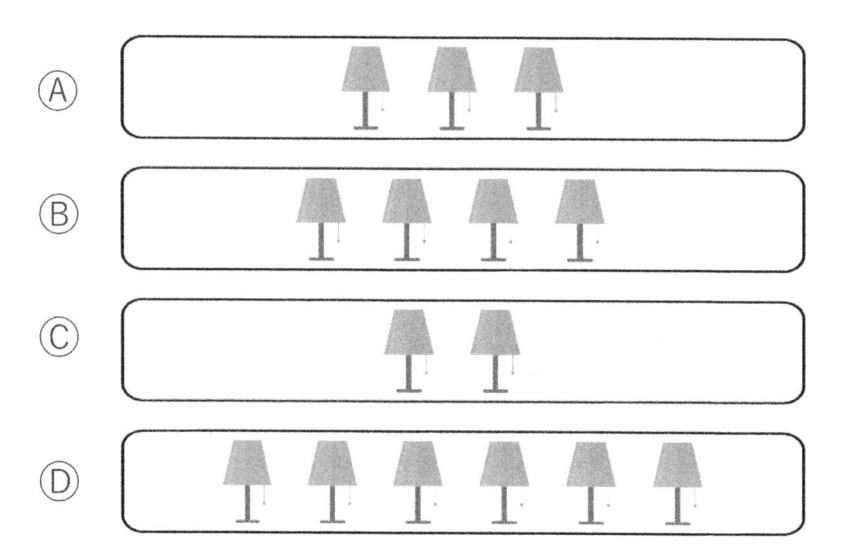

Ⓐ [3 lamps]

Ⓑ [4 lamps]

Ⓒ [2 lamps]

Ⓓ [6 lamps]

2. How many fingers are held up?

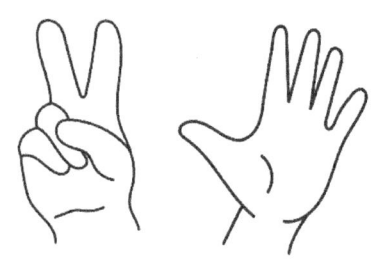

Ⓐ 4

Ⓑ 5

Ⓒ 6

Ⓓ 7

3 What number is added to 6 to make 10?

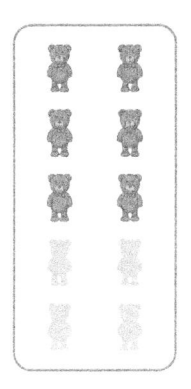

- Ⓐ 2
- Ⓑ 3
- Ⓒ 4
- Ⓓ 5

4 Which of these describes the ball?

- Ⓐ heavier than the bag
- Ⓑ lighter than the bag
- Ⓒ longer than the bag
- Ⓓ taller than the bag

5 What do the four triangles make?

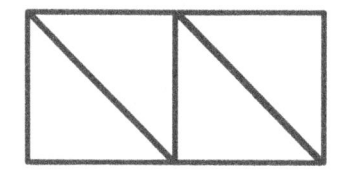

- Ⓐ circle
- Ⓑ rectangle
- Ⓒ square
- Ⓓ triangle

6 Which shaped lock is there 5 of?

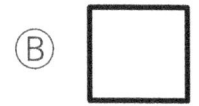

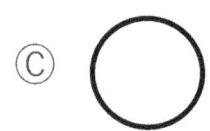

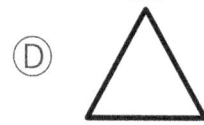

- Ⓐ heart
- Ⓑ square
- Ⓒ circle
- Ⓓ triangle

Warm-Up

Practice Set 6

Instructions

Read each question carefully.

Each question has four answer choices.

Fill in the circle for the correct answer.

1   Which card has 4 sharks on it?

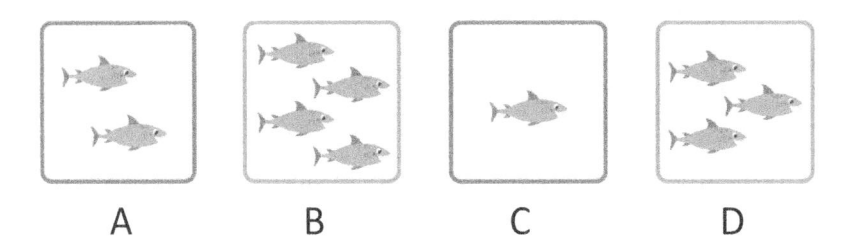

| A | B | C | D |

- Ⓐ   Card A
- Ⓑ   Card B
- Ⓒ   Card C
- Ⓓ   Card D

2   Which number is 1 less than 17?

- Ⓐ   15
- Ⓑ   16
- Ⓒ   18
- Ⓓ   19

3 Which of these shows 4 cows?

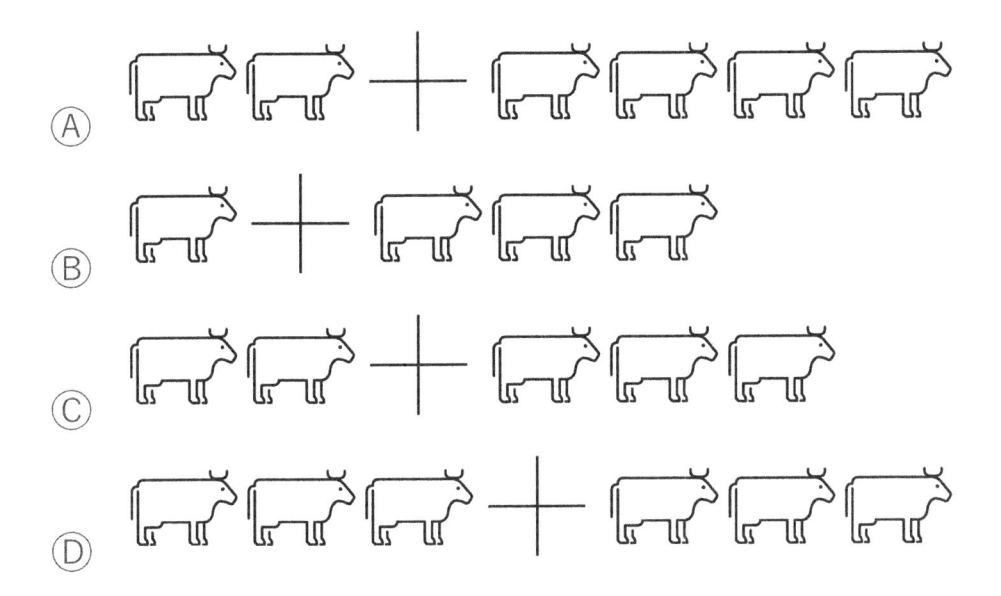

Ⓐ
Ⓑ
Ⓒ
Ⓓ

4 How tall is the dollhouse?

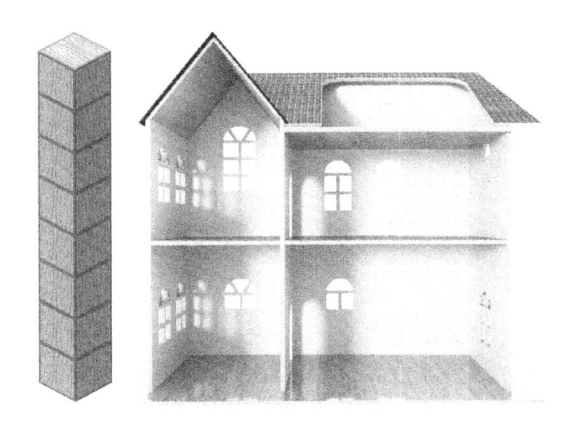

Ⓐ 4 blocks

Ⓑ 6 blocks

Ⓒ 8 blocks

Ⓓ 10 blocks

5 Which shape is a cone?

Ⓐ (cylinder)

Ⓑ (cone)

Ⓒ (cube)

Ⓓ (sphere)

6 How many flags are shaped like triangles?

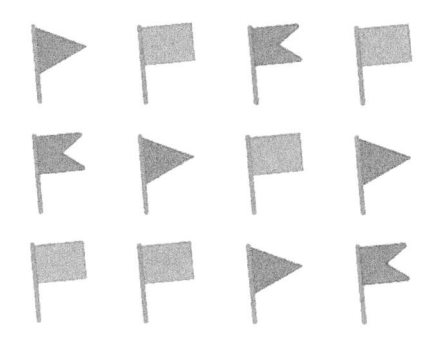

Ⓐ 4
Ⓑ 5
Ⓒ 7
Ⓓ 8

Warm-Up

Practice Set 7

Instructions

Read each question carefully.

Each question has four answer choices.

Fill in the circle for the correct answer.

1   Which animal is third in the line?

Ⓐ cat
Ⓑ cow
Ⓒ dog
Ⓓ horse

2   Which number is shown below?

$$1 \text{ ten} + 8 \text{ ones}$$

Ⓐ 9
Ⓑ 18
Ⓒ 19
Ⓓ 81

3 Meg had 6 eggs.

She used 2 eggs to make a cake. How many are left?

Ⓐ 2 eggs
Ⓑ 3 eggs
Ⓒ 4 eggs
Ⓓ 5 eggs

4 What is being found about the watermelon?

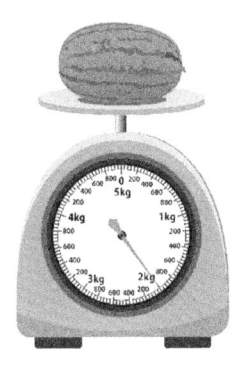

Ⓐ how long it is
Ⓑ how heavy it is
Ⓒ how tall it is
Ⓓ how empty it is

5 What do all the shapes have?

Ⓐ equal sides
Ⓑ curved sides
Ⓒ four sides
Ⓓ straight sides

6 Which shape are 3 of the balloons?

Ⓐ circles
Ⓑ hearts
Ⓒ rabbits
Ⓓ ovals

Warm-Up

Practice Set 8

Instructions

Read each question carefully.

Each question has four answer choices.

Fill in the circle for the correct answer.

1 Which set has the most books?

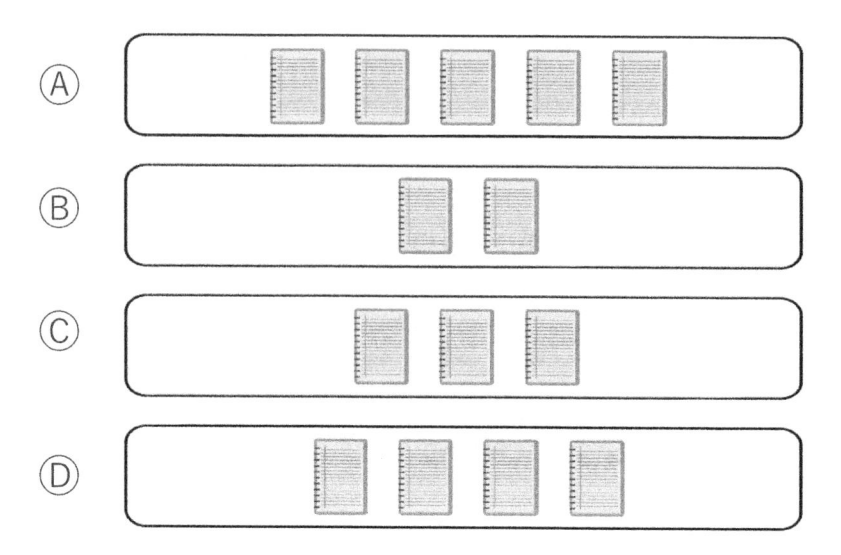

Ⓐ
Ⓑ
Ⓒ
Ⓓ

2 Which number is less than 14?

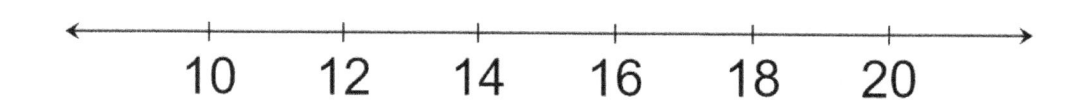

Ⓐ 12
Ⓑ 16
Ⓒ 18
Ⓓ 20

3 What is 6 − 3?

$6 - 3 = \,?$

Ⓐ 3
Ⓑ 4
Ⓒ 8
Ⓓ 9

4 Which pot holds the most?

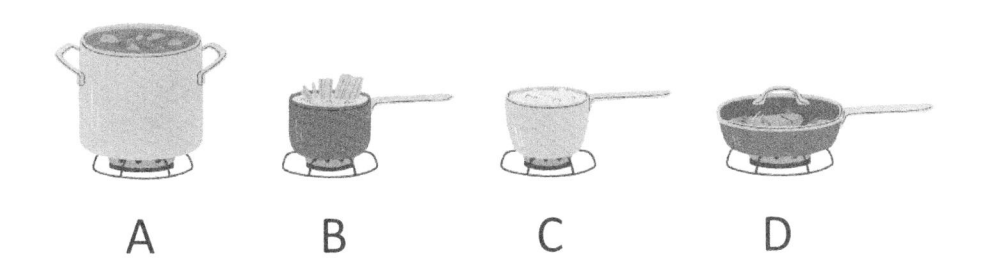

A   B   C   D

Ⓐ Pot A
Ⓑ Pot B
Ⓒ Pot C
Ⓓ Pot D

5 Which shape has square faces?

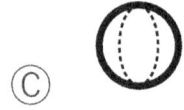

Ⓐ cone

Ⓑ cube

Ⓒ sphere

Ⓓ cylinder

6 Which shape is there the most of?

Ⓐ circle

Ⓑ rectangle

Ⓒ square

Ⓓ triangle

Warm-Up

Practice Set 9

Instructions

Read each question carefully.

Each question has four answer choices.

Fill in the circle for the correct answer.

1 Which set has the same number of flowers?

Ⓐ
Ⓑ
Ⓒ
Ⓓ

2 What is 6 – 2?

Ⓐ 3
Ⓑ 4
Ⓒ 7
Ⓓ 8

3 What number is added to 8 to make 10?

Ⓐ 2

Ⓑ 4

Ⓒ 7

Ⓓ 9

4 Abby placed some bricks along a garden. How long is the garden?

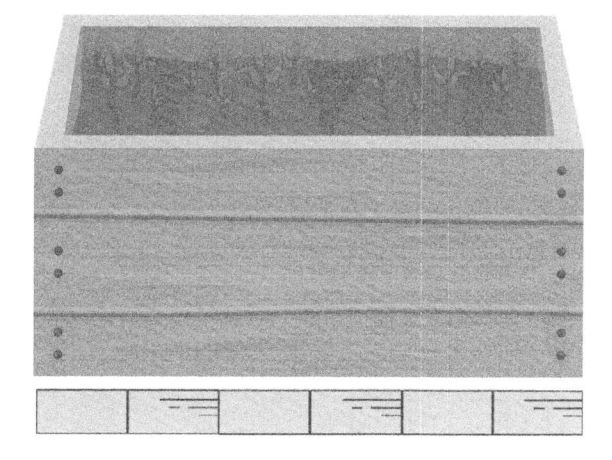

Ⓐ 4 bricks

Ⓑ 5 bricks

Ⓒ 6 bricks

Ⓓ 7 bricks

5 Which item is shaped like a cube?

Ⓐ dice

Ⓑ donut

Ⓒ cake

Ⓓ football

6 Which shows how many books there are?

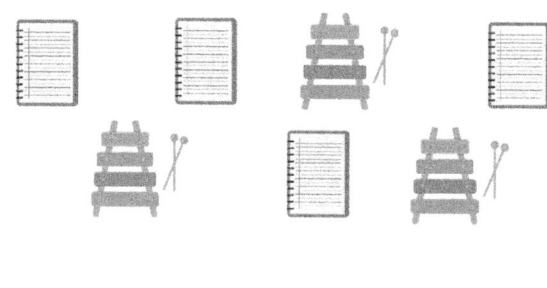

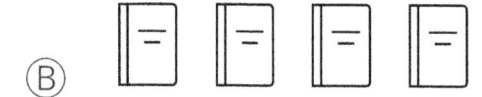

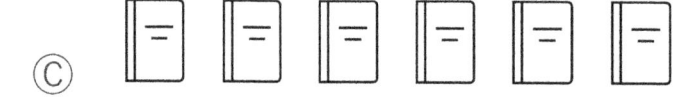

Ⓐ
Ⓑ
Ⓒ
Ⓓ

Warm-Up

Practice Set 10

Instructions

Read each question carefully.

Each question has four answer choices.

Fill in the circle for the correct answer.

FAST Mathematics Skills Workbook, Daily Star Practice, Kindergarten

1   In what place is the clock?

   Ⓐ   second
   Ⓑ   third
   Ⓒ   fourth
   Ⓓ   fifth

2   Which number is 3 less than 9?

   Ⓐ   4
   Ⓑ   5
   Ⓒ   6
   Ⓓ   7

3 There are 4 tomatoes.

Then 2 tomatoes are eaten. How many tomatoes are left?

Ⓐ 1
Ⓑ 2
Ⓒ 6
Ⓓ 7

4 Which measure tells how much the juice box holds?

Ⓐ cost
Ⓑ height
Ⓒ volume
Ⓓ weight

5 How many small squares make up the rectangle?

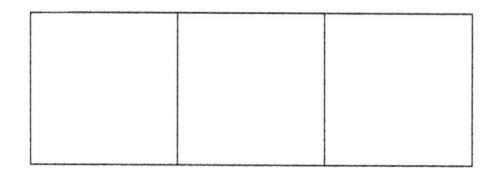

Ⓐ 2
Ⓑ 3
Ⓒ 4
Ⓓ 5

6 Which set has 3 spotted mushrooms and 2 plain mushrooms?

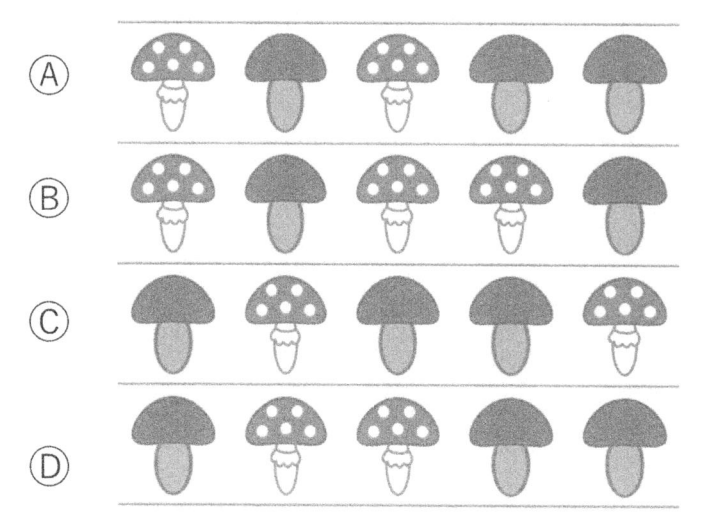

FAST Mathematics Skills Workbook, Daily Star Practice, Kindergarten

Mini Practice Tests

Practice Set 11

Instructions

Read each question carefully.

Each question has four answer choices.

Fill in the circle for the correct answer.

1   How many balloons are there?

(A) 6
(B) 7
(C) 8
(D) 9

2   Which number is sixty-eight?

(A) 66
(B) 67
(C) 68
(D) 69

3 What is 9 − 7?

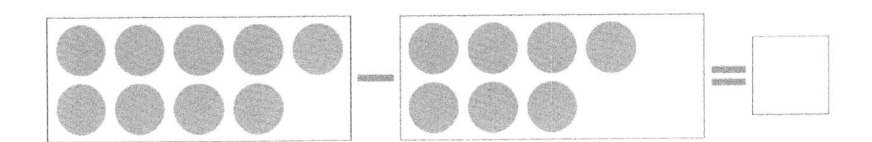

Ⓐ 1
Ⓑ 2
Ⓒ 3
Ⓓ 4

4 What number is added to 2 to make 10?

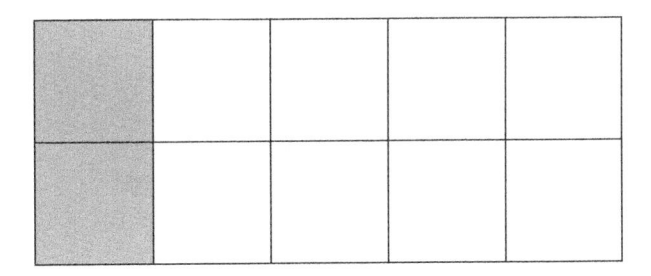

Ⓐ 6
Ⓑ 7
Ⓒ 8
Ⓓ 9

5   What does the picture show?

$$\text{🌴🌴🌴} + \text{🌴🌴} = \boxed{?}$$

   Ⓐ   2 + 2 = 4
   Ⓑ   2 + 5 = 7
   Ⓒ   3 + 2 = 5
   Ⓓ   3 + 5 = 8

6   What is this showing about the bananas?

   Ⓐ   cost
   Ⓑ   length
   Ⓒ   volume
   Ⓓ   weight

7 How long is the paintbrush?

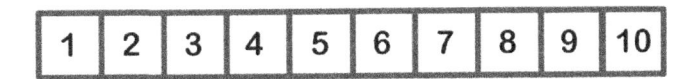

| 1 | 2 | 3 | 4 | 5 | 6 | 7 | 8 | 9 | 10 |

- Ⓐ 3 units
- Ⓑ 4 units
- Ⓒ 5 units
- Ⓓ 6 units

8 What shapes are shown?

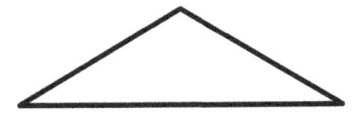

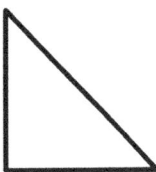

- Ⓐ circles
- Ⓑ rectangles
- Ⓒ squares
- Ⓓ triangles

9 What is the large triangle made of?

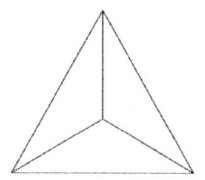

- Ⓐ 2 small triangles
- Ⓑ 3 small triangles
- Ⓒ 2 small rectangles
- Ⓓ 3 small rectangles

10 How many boats are there?

- Ⓐ 4
- Ⓑ 5
- Ⓒ 6
- Ⓓ 7

Mini Practice Tests

Practice Set 12

Instructions

Read each question carefully.

Each question has four answer choices.

Fill in the circle for the correct answer.

1 Which set has 9 caps?

Ⓐ 🧢🧢🧢🧢🧢🧢

Ⓑ 🧢🧢🧢🧢🧢🧢🧢

Ⓒ 🧢🧢🧢🧢🧢🧢🧢🧢

Ⓓ 🧢🧢🧢🧢🧢🧢🧢🧢🧢

2 What number is shown?

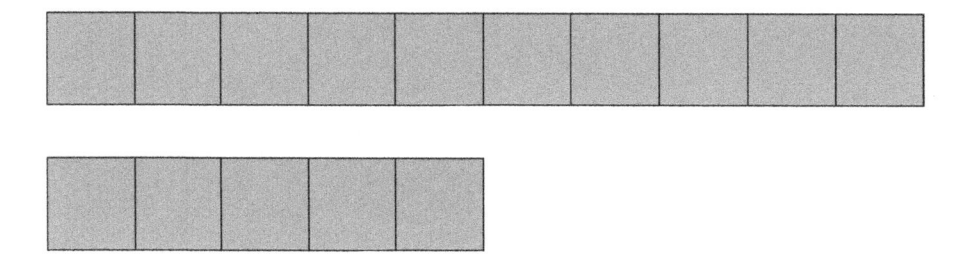

Ⓐ 1 ten + 5 ones

Ⓑ 1 ten + 15 ones

Ⓒ 10 tens + 5 ones

Ⓓ 10 tens + 15 ones

3 How many fingers are held up?

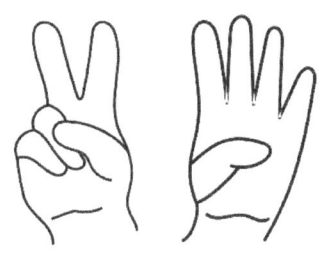

Ⓐ 4
Ⓑ 5
Ⓒ 6
Ⓓ 7

4 What is equal to 8?

Ⓐ 3 + 3
Ⓑ 3 + 4
Ⓒ 3 + 5
Ⓓ 3 + 6

5 What is 4 − 3?

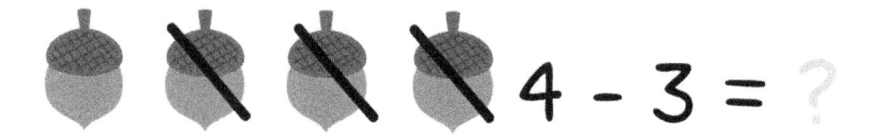

$$4 - 3 = \;?$$

- Ⓐ 1
- Ⓑ 2
- Ⓒ 7
- Ⓓ 8

6 Which pencil is the tallest?

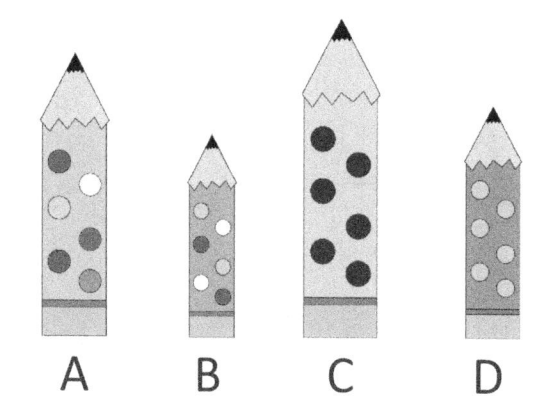

A B C D

- Ⓐ Pencil A
- Ⓑ Pencil B
- Ⓒ Pencil C
- Ⓓ Pencil D

7 Henry places some tuna cans next to a soda. How tall is the soda?

- Ⓐ 2 cans
- Ⓑ 3 cans
- Ⓒ 4 cans
- Ⓓ 5 cans

8 Which item is shaped like a triangle?

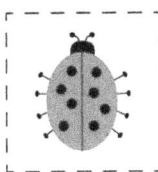

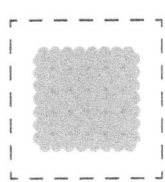

- Ⓐ hat
- Ⓑ beetle
- Ⓒ bag
- Ⓓ cookie

9 Which shape has 3 sides?

- Ⓐ circle
- Ⓑ square
- Ⓒ rectangle
- Ⓓ triangle

10 Which item are there 4 of?

- Ⓐ cup
- Ⓑ kettle
- Ⓒ plate
- Ⓓ pot

Mini Practice Tests

Practice Set 13

Instructions

Read each question carefully.

Each question has four answer choices.

Fill in the circle for the correct answer.

FAST Mathematics Skills Workbook, Daily Star Practice, Kindergarten

1   Which object is fourth in the line?

Ⓐ bag
Ⓑ bee
Ⓒ box
Ⓓ egg

2   Which number goes in the box?

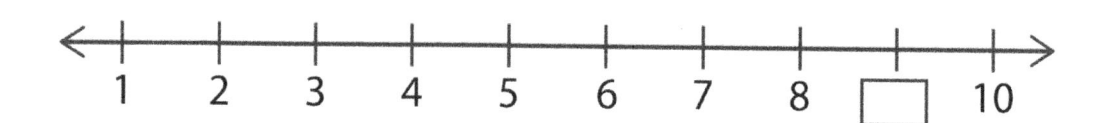

Ⓐ 6
Ⓑ 7
Ⓒ 8
Ⓓ 9

3 What is 3 + 4?

- Ⓐ 5
- Ⓑ 6
- Ⓒ 7
- Ⓓ 8

4 There were 4 rabbits in a field. Then 4 more rabbits ran in.

How many rabbits are there in all?

- Ⓐ 7
- Ⓑ 8
- Ⓒ 9
- Ⓓ 10

5 Which picture shows 2 + 1 = 3?

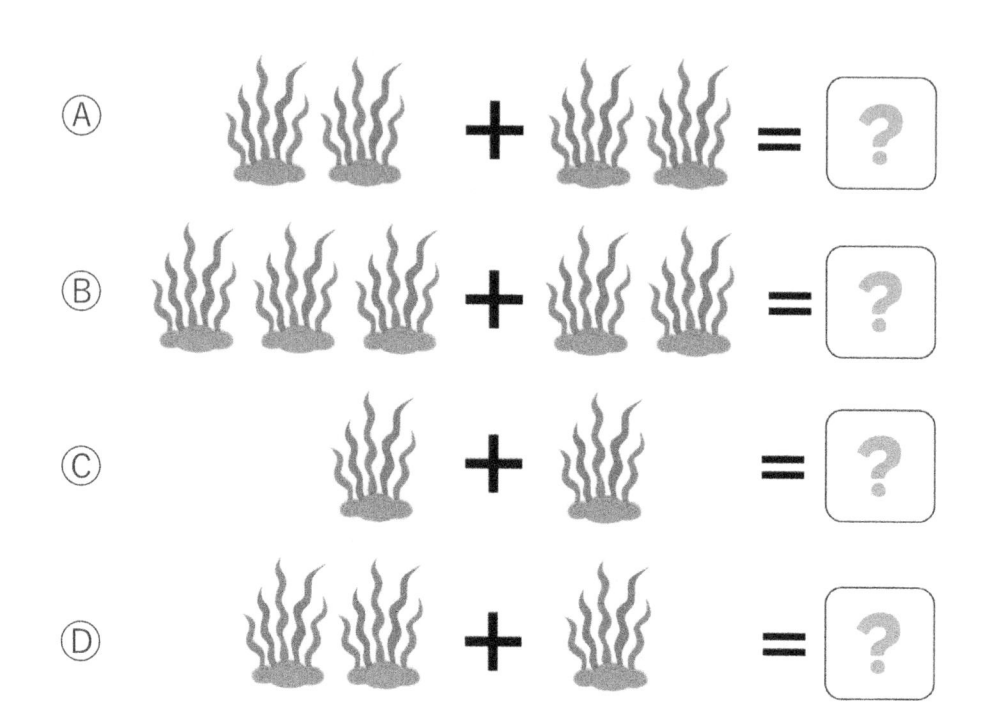

Ⓐ 🌿🌿 + 🌿🌿 = ?

Ⓑ 🌿🌿🌿 + 🌿🌿 = ?

Ⓒ 🌿 + 🌿 = ?

Ⓓ 🌿🌿 + 🌿 = ?

6 Which tells how much water the bucket can hold?

Ⓐ height
Ⓑ length
Ⓒ volume
Ⓓ weight

7 How long is the toothbrush?

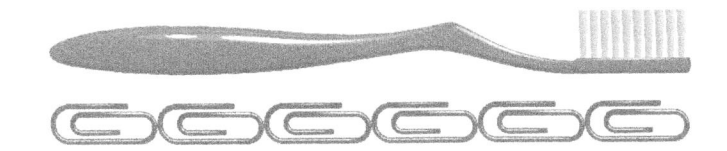

Ⓐ 4
Ⓑ 5
Ⓒ 6
Ⓓ 7

8 Which shape is a cube?

Ⓐ
Ⓑ
Ⓒ
Ⓓ

9 Which of these describes a cone?

- Ⓐ no round faces
- Ⓑ 1 round face
- Ⓒ 2 round faces
- Ⓓ 3 round faces

10 Which shape is there the most of?

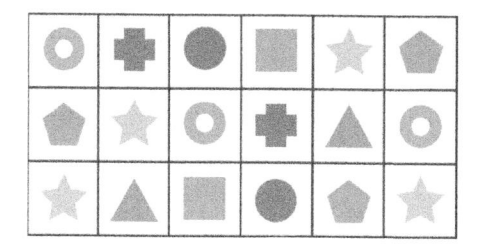

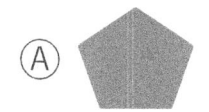

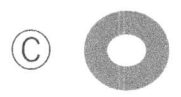

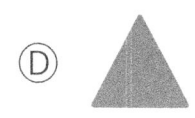

- Ⓐ pentagon
- Ⓑ star
- Ⓒ circle
- Ⓓ triangle

Mini Practice Tests

Practice Set 14

Instructions

Read each question carefully.

Each question has four answer choices.

Fill in the circle for the correct answer.

1. In which set are there more planes than buses?

    Ⓐ ✈ ✈ ✈ ✈ 🚌 🚌

    Ⓑ ✈ 🚌 🚌 🚌 🚌 🚌

    Ⓒ ✈ ✈ ✈ 🚌 🚌 🚌

    Ⓓ ✈ ✈ 🚌 🚌 🚌 🚌

2. Which number comes right after 53?

    Ⓐ 54
    Ⓑ 55
    Ⓒ 56
    Ⓓ 57

3 Which number is 4 more than 3?

- Ⓐ 6
- Ⓑ 7
- Ⓒ 8
- Ⓓ 9

4 What number is added to 7 to make 10?

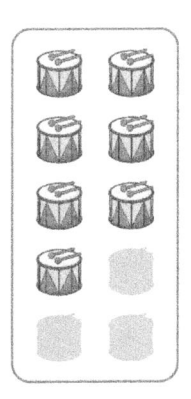

- Ⓐ 2
- Ⓑ 3
- Ⓒ 4
- Ⓓ 5

5 What does the picture show?

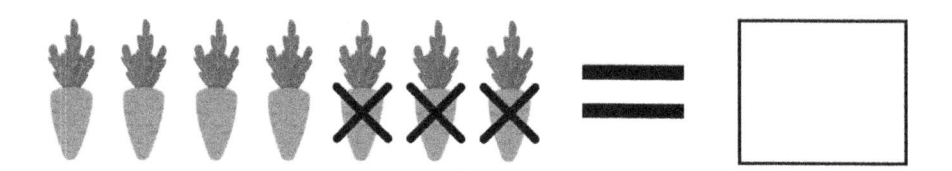

Ⓐ 7 − 3 = 4
Ⓑ 7 − 4 = 4
Ⓒ 4 + 4 = 7
Ⓓ 7 + 3 = 10

6 How is the jug different from the cup?

Ⓐ It holds more.
Ⓑ It weighs less.
Ⓒ It is emptier.
Ⓓ It is shorter.

7 How tall is the milk bottle?

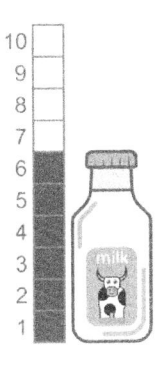

Ⓐ 4 units

Ⓑ 6 units

Ⓒ 8 units

Ⓓ 10 units

8 What is the can shaped like?

Ⓐ cone

Ⓑ cube

Ⓒ cylinder

Ⓓ sphere

9 What do the triangles combine to make?

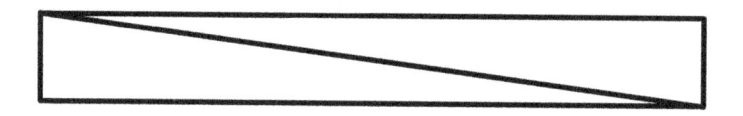

Ⓐ circle
Ⓑ square
Ⓒ rectangle
Ⓓ triangle

10 Which shows how many square buttons there are?

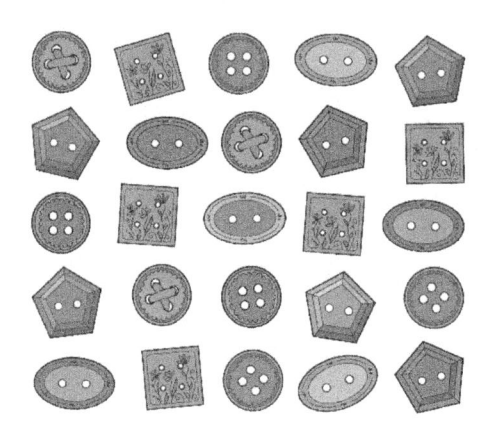

Ⓐ
Ⓑ
Ⓒ
Ⓓ

Mini Practice Tests

Practice Set 15

Instructions

Read each question carefully.

Each question has four answer choices.

Fill in the circle for the correct answer.

FAST Mathematics Skills Workbook, Daily Star Practice, Kindergarten

1. Which set has 7 buttons?

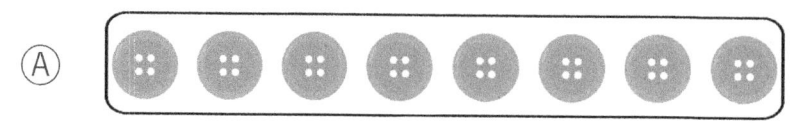

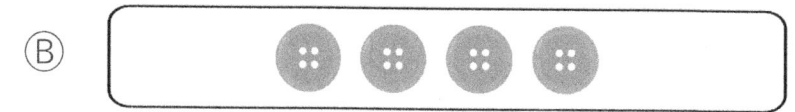

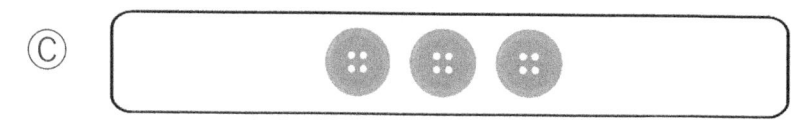

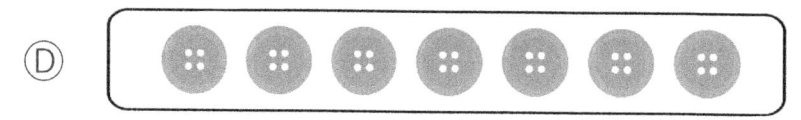

Ⓐ (8 buttons)
Ⓑ (4 buttons)
Ⓒ (3 buttons)
Ⓓ (7 buttons)

2. Which number is shown below?

1 ten + 2 ones

Ⓐ 3
Ⓑ 12
Ⓒ 13
Ⓓ 21

3 Which shows 2 less than 8?

Ⓐ 2 – 8

Ⓑ 8 – 2

Ⓒ 2 + 8

Ⓓ 8 + 2

4 Which of these shows 7 buttons?

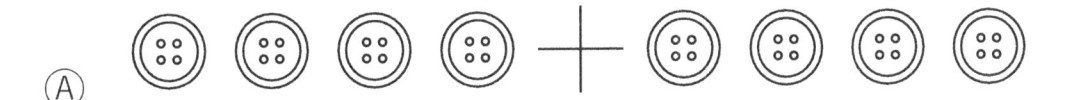

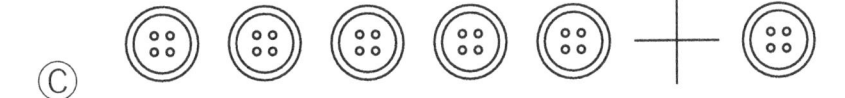

Ⓐ
Ⓑ
Ⓒ
Ⓓ

5 What do the shaded squares show?

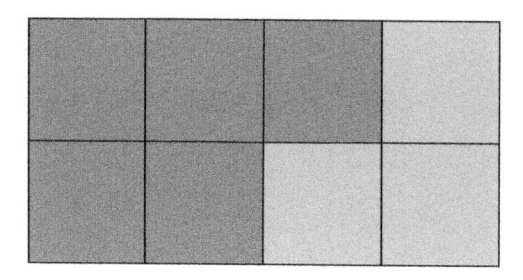

- Ⓐ 3 + 5 = 7
- Ⓑ 3 + 5 = 8
- Ⓒ 3 + 5 = 9
- Ⓓ 3 + 5 = 10

6 What does 7 meters tell about the shark?

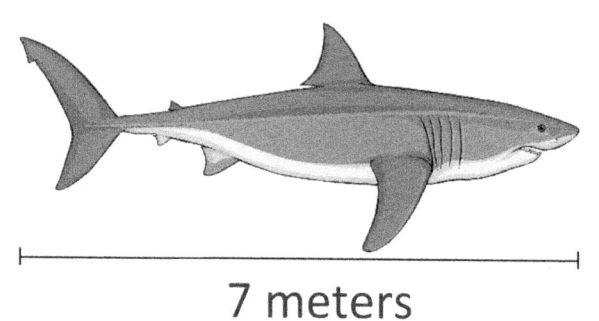

7 meters

- Ⓐ how heavy it is
- Ⓑ how old it is
- Ⓒ how long it is
- Ⓓ how fast it is

7 The picture shows how many clipboards fit across a shelf. How long is the shelf?

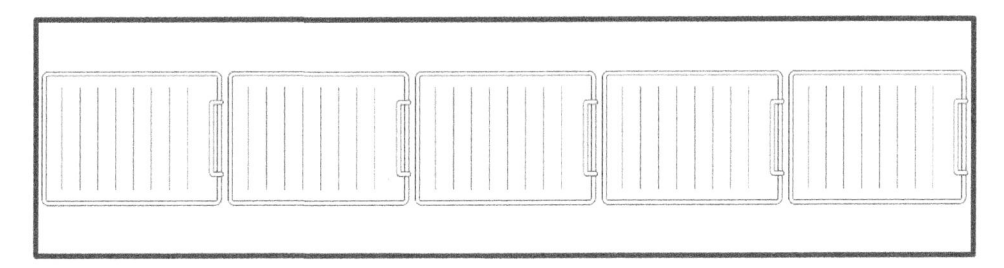

Ⓐ 3 clipboards

Ⓑ 4 clipboards

Ⓒ 5 clipboards

Ⓓ 6 clipboards

8 Which shape is a square?

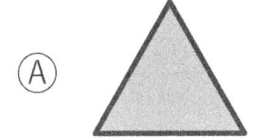

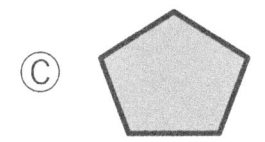

Ⓐ

Ⓑ

Ⓒ

Ⓓ

9 Which two shapes are the same size?

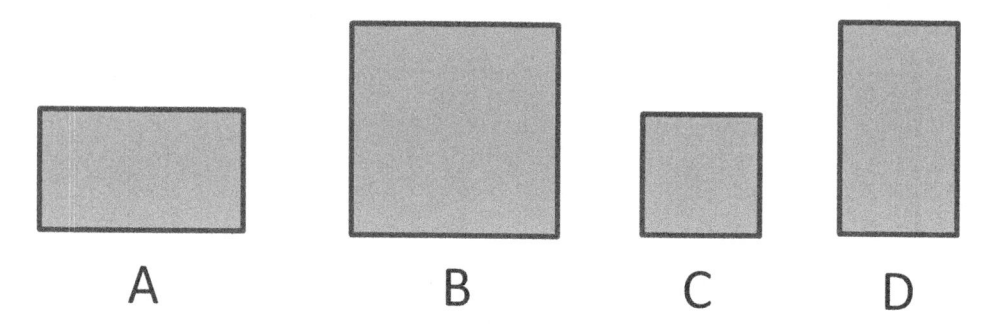

A B C D

Ⓐ Shapes A and C
Ⓑ Shapes B and C
Ⓒ Shapes A and D
Ⓓ Shapes B and D

10 Which item is there 9 of?

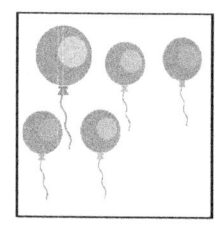

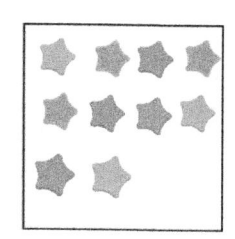

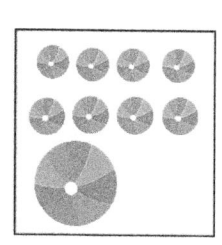

Ⓐ balloon
Ⓑ cup
Ⓒ star
Ⓓ ball

Mini Practice Tests

Practice Set 16

Instructions

Read each question carefully.

Each question has four answer choices.

Fill in the circle for the correct answer.

1. Which card has 5 tacks on it?

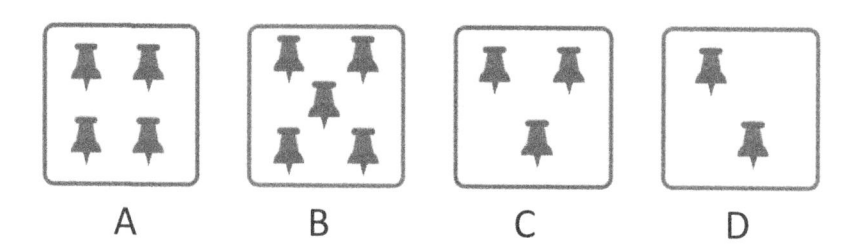

  A   B   C   D

  Ⓐ Card A
  Ⓑ Card B
  Ⓒ Card C
  Ⓓ Card D

2. Which number is greater than 16?

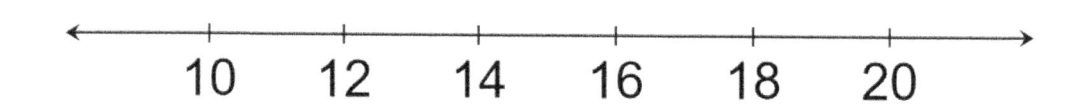

  10 12 14 16 18 20

  Ⓐ 10
  Ⓑ 12
  Ⓒ 14
  Ⓓ 18

3 What is the sum of 4 and 5?

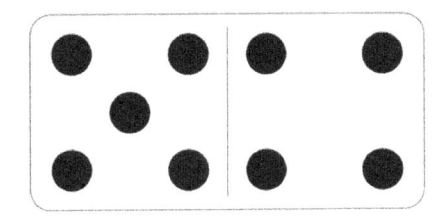

Ⓐ 7
Ⓑ 8
Ⓒ 9
Ⓓ 10

4 There are 9 cakes.

Then 2 cakes are eaten. How many cakes are left?

Ⓐ 5
Ⓑ 6
Ⓒ 7
Ⓓ 8

5   What does the picture show?

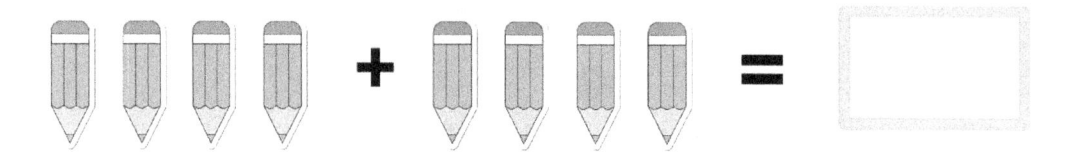

      ✏️✏️✏️✏️ + ✏️✏️✏️✏️ = ☐

   Ⓐ 2 + 2 = 4
   Ⓑ 3 + 3 = 6
   Ⓒ 4 + 4 = 8
   Ⓓ 5 + 5 = 10

6   How is the watermelon different from the apple?

   Ⓐ It is shorter.
   Ⓑ It is heavier.
   Ⓒ It is higher.
   Ⓓ It is lighter.

FAST Mathematics Skills Workbook, Daily Star Practice, Kindergarten

7 How long are the scissors?

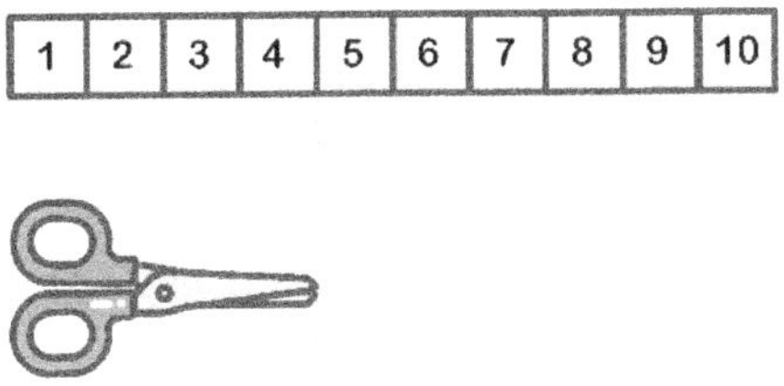

Ⓐ 3 units
Ⓑ 4 units
Ⓒ 5 units
Ⓓ 6 units

8 Which item is shaped like a rectangle?

A B C D

Ⓐ chessboard
Ⓑ letter
Ⓒ clock
Ⓓ sign

9   What shapes are shown below?

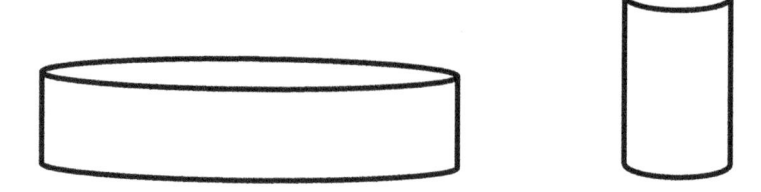

- Ⓐ two cones
- Ⓑ two cylinders
- Ⓒ a cylinder and a cone
- Ⓓ a cone and a sphere

10 How many boots are there?

- Ⓐ 3
- Ⓑ 4
- Ⓒ 5
- Ⓓ 6

Mini Practice Tests

Practice Set 17

Instructions

Read each question carefully.

Each question has four answer choices.

Fill in the circle for the correct answer.

1   In what place is the kite?

- Ⓐ second
- Ⓑ third
- Ⓒ fourth
- Ⓓ fifth

2   Which number is fifty-seven?

- Ⓐ 54
- Ⓑ 55
- Ⓒ 56
- Ⓓ 57

3   What is 8 − 5?

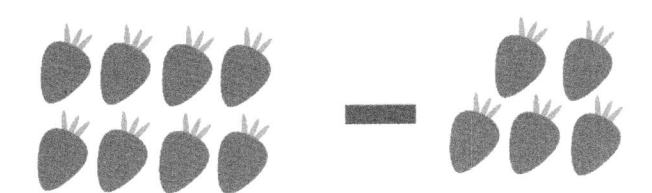

Ⓐ 1
Ⓑ 2
Ⓒ 3
Ⓓ 4

4   What number is added to 5 to make 10?

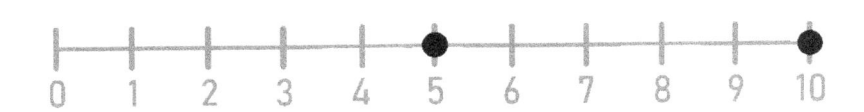

Ⓐ 3
Ⓑ 5
Ⓒ 7
Ⓓ 9

5 What does the picture show?

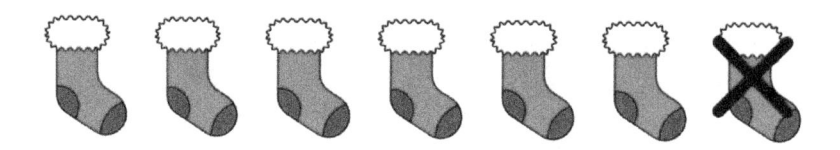

Ⓐ 7 − 1 = 6

Ⓑ 8 − 1 = 7

Ⓒ 7 + 1 = 8

Ⓓ 8 + 1 = 9

6 What is being found about the apples?

Ⓐ how heavy they are

Ⓑ how many there are

Ⓒ how hard they are

Ⓓ how long they are

7 Joe finds how many steps long a ladder is. How long is the ladder?

Ⓐ 4 steps

Ⓑ 5 steps

Ⓒ 6 steps

Ⓓ 7 steps

8 What shape is shown?

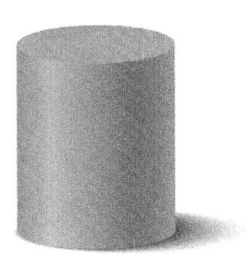

Ⓐ cone

Ⓑ cube

Ⓒ cylinder

Ⓓ sphere

9 Which shows two rectangles forming a square?

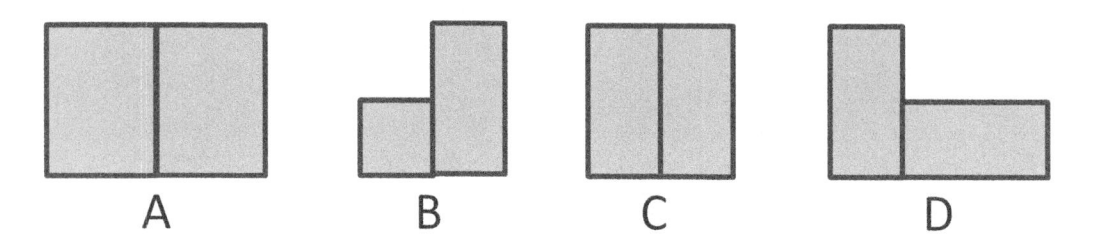

  A B C D

- Ⓐ Shape A
- Ⓑ Shape B
- Ⓒ Shape C
- Ⓓ Shape D

10 Which item are there 7 of?

- Ⓐ bags
- Ⓑ books
- Ⓒ pencils
- Ⓓ rulers

Mini Practice Tests

Practice Set 18

Instructions

Read each question carefully.

Each question has four answer choices.

Fill in the circle for the correct answer.

FAST Mathematics Skills Workbook, Daily Star Practice, Kindergarten

1 Which set has fewer than 3 lemons?

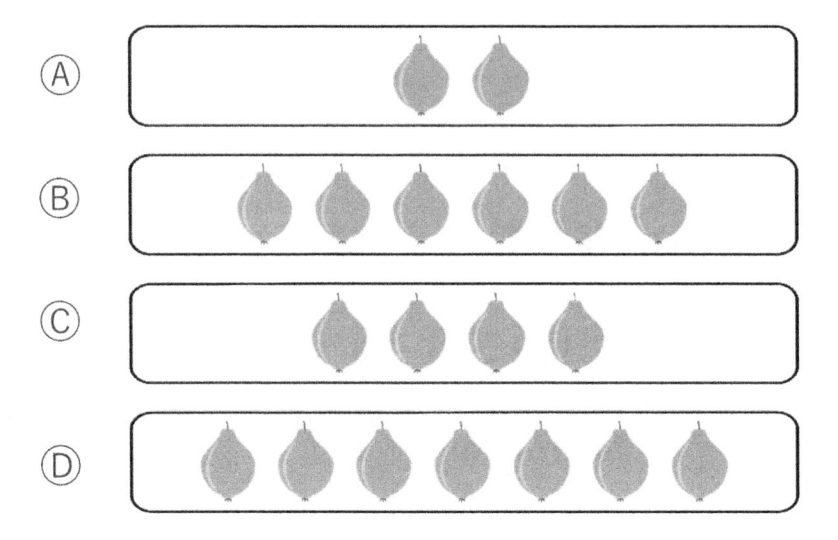

2 What number do the blocks show?

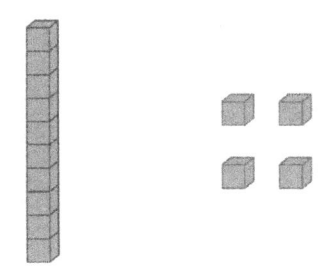

Ⓐ 14

Ⓑ 40

Ⓒ 41

Ⓓ 44

3 What is 5 − 3?

Ⓐ 1
Ⓑ 2
Ⓒ 7
Ⓓ 8

4 Which is equal to 7?

Ⓐ 2 + 3
Ⓑ 2 + 4
Ⓒ 2 + 5
Ⓓ 2 + 6

5 Which picture shows 2 + 2 = 4?

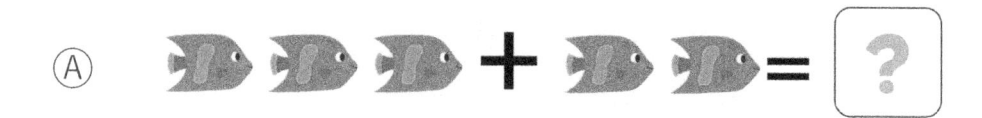

Ⓐ 🐟🐟🐟 + 🐟🐟 = ❓

Ⓑ 🐟🐟 + 🐟🐟 = ❓

Ⓒ 🐟🐟 + 🐟 = ❓

Ⓓ 🐟 + 🐟 = ❓

6 Which of these describes the train?

Ⓐ heavier than the car

Ⓑ lighter than the car

Ⓒ shorter than the car

Ⓓ longer than the car

7 A park has the fences below on each side.

How long is the park?

Ⓐ 4 fences
Ⓑ 6 fences
Ⓒ 8 fences
Ⓓ 10 fences

8 What are the two objects shaped like?

Ⓐ cones
Ⓑ cubes
Ⓒ cylinders
Ⓓ spheres

9   Which shape has 4 equal sides?

   Ⓐ circle
   Ⓑ rectangle
   Ⓒ square
   Ⓓ triangle

10 Which shape is there the most of?

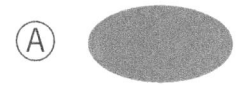

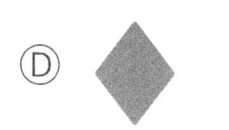

   Ⓐ (oval)
   Ⓑ (triangle)
   Ⓒ (rectangle)
   Ⓓ (diamond)

Mini Practice Tests

Practice Set 19

Instructions

Read each question carefully.

Each question has four answer choices.

Fill in the circle for the correct answer.

1 Which set has the same number of lollipops?

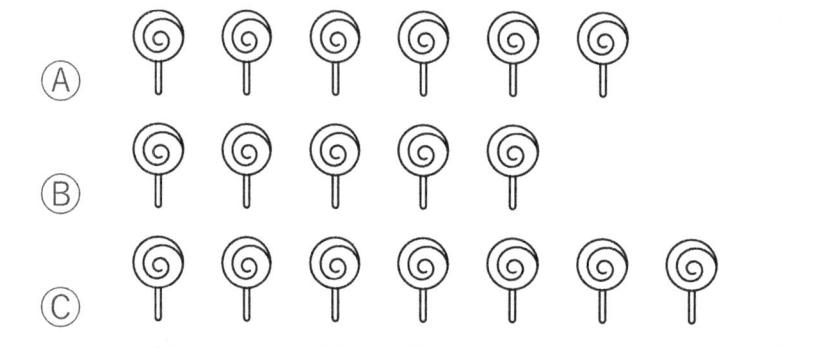

- Ⓐ (6 lollipops)
- Ⓑ (5 lollipops)
- Ⓒ (7 lollipops)
- Ⓓ (8 lollipops)

2 What does the number line show?

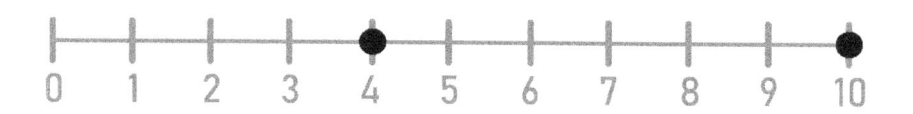

- Ⓐ 4 is equal to 10
- Ⓑ 4 is less than 10
- Ⓒ 4 is more than 10
- Ⓓ 4 is greater than 10

3 What is 3 less than 9?

|—|—|—|—|—|—|—|—|—|—|—|
0 1 2 3 4 5 6 7 8 9 10

Ⓐ 5

Ⓑ 6

Ⓒ 7

Ⓓ 8

4 There are 8 balloons.

Then 4 balloons pop. How many balloons are left?

Ⓐ 2

Ⓑ 3

Ⓒ 4

Ⓓ 5

5 What do the shaded squares show?

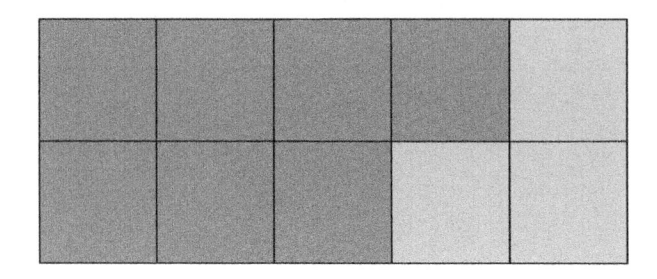

Ⓐ 7 + 3 = 7

Ⓑ 7 + 3 = 8

Ⓒ 7 + 3 = 9

Ⓓ 7 + 3 = 10

6 What does 10 liters tell about the jug?

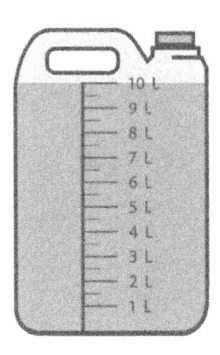

10-liter jug

Ⓐ how heavy it is

Ⓑ how tall it is

Ⓒ how much it costs

Ⓓ how much it holds

7 How tall is the hammer?

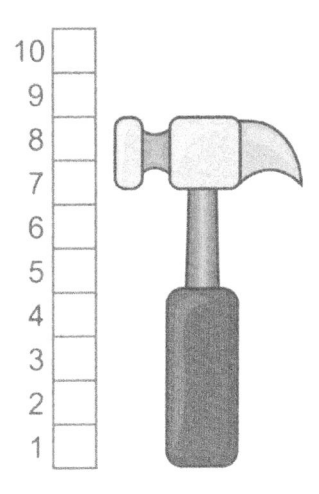

Ⓐ 4 units

Ⓑ 6 units

Ⓒ 8 units

Ⓓ 10 units

8 What are both shapes?

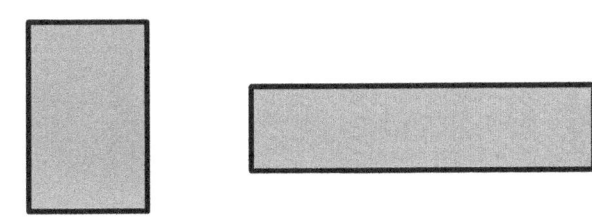

Ⓐ circles

Ⓑ squares

Ⓒ rectangles

Ⓓ triangles

9   Which shape does not have any curved sides?

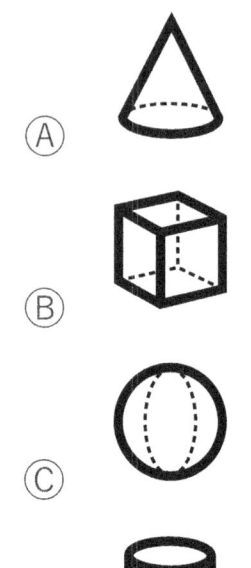

Ⓐ

Ⓑ

Ⓒ

Ⓓ

10   How many shirts are on the line?

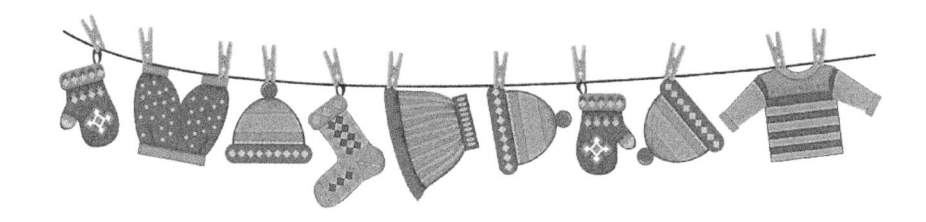

Ⓐ 1
Ⓑ 2
Ⓒ 3
Ⓓ 4

Mini Practice Tests

Practice Set 20

Instructions

Read each question carefully.

Each question has four answer choices.

Fill in the circle for the correct answer.

FAST Mathematics Skills Workbook, Daily Star Practice, Kindergarten

1. Which object is third in the line?

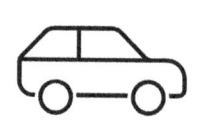

- Ⓐ apple
- Ⓑ barn
- Ⓒ button
- Ⓓ car

2. Which number is 1 more than 59?

- Ⓐ 50
- Ⓑ 60
- Ⓒ 70
- Ⓓ 80

3 What is 5 + 2?

Ⓐ 5
Ⓑ 6
Ⓒ 7
Ⓓ 8

4 What number is added to 3 to make 10?

Ⓐ 3
Ⓑ 5
Ⓒ 7
Ⓓ 9

5 Which picture shows 6 − 3 = 3?

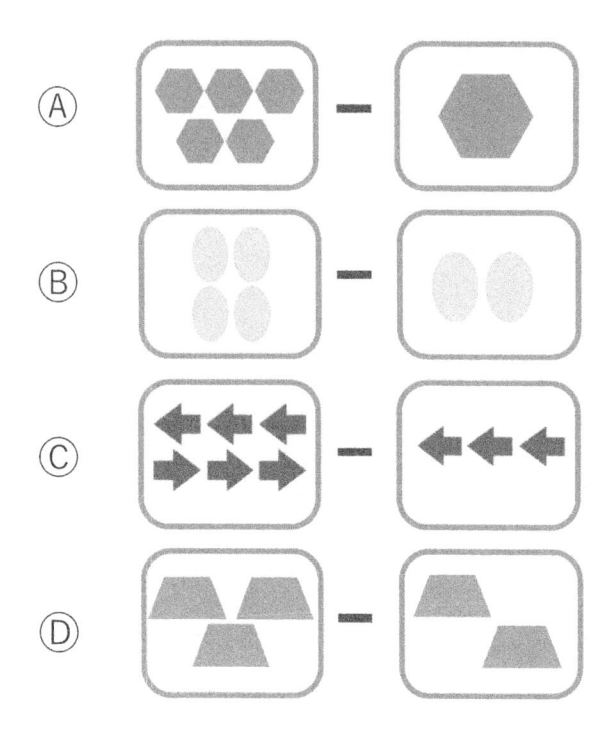

Ⓐ ⬡⬡⬡ ⬡⬡ − ⬡

Ⓑ (4 ovals) − (2 ovals)

Ⓒ (6 arrows) − (3 arrows)

Ⓓ (3 trapezoids) − (2 trapezoids)

6 Which cylinder is the most full?

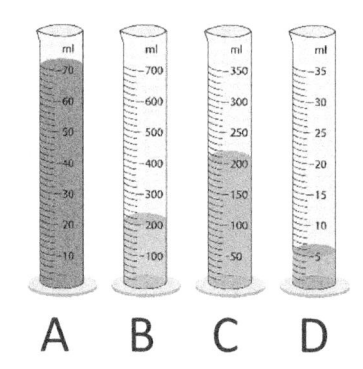

A   B   C   D

Ⓐ Cylinder A
Ⓑ Cylinder B
Ⓒ Cylinder B
Ⓓ Cylinder D

7 Adam throws a ball. He lays out baseball bats to find how far he threw it.

How far did he throw the ball?

Ⓐ 1
Ⓑ 2
Ⓒ 3
Ⓓ 4

8 What is the pizza shaped like?

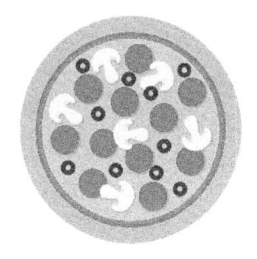

Ⓐ circle
Ⓑ rectangle
Ⓒ square
Ⓓ triangle

9 Which shows two triangles forming a square?

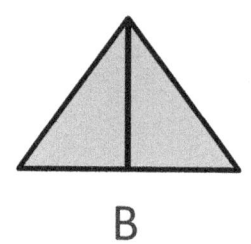

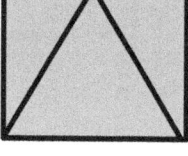

A   B   C   D

- Ⓐ Shape A
- Ⓑ Shape B
- Ⓒ Shape C
- Ⓓ Shape D

10 Which set has 2 suns and 4 raindrops?

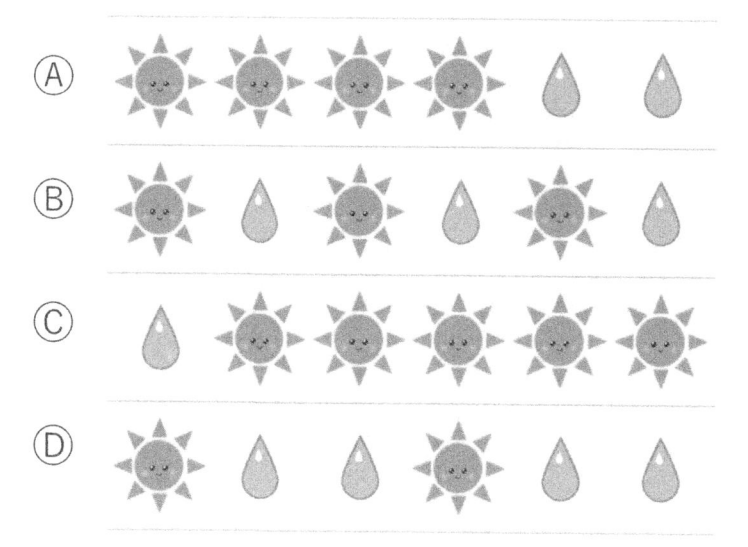

- Ⓐ
- Ⓑ
- Ⓒ
- Ⓓ

ANSWER KEY

Introducing the B.E.S.T. Standards for Mathematics

In 2020, the state of Florida introduced the B.E.S.T. standards. The standards describe the skills and knowledge that students are expected to have. The new standards will be fully introduced by 2022-2023 and the state tests will assess these new standards beginning with the 2022-2023 school year.

About the B.E.S.T. Standards for Mathematics

The B.E.S.T. Standards for Kindergarten are divided into five strands, or topics. These are listed below.

- Number Sense and Operations
- Algebraic Reasoning
- Measurement
- Geometric Reasoning
- Data Analysis and Probability

Within each strand, there is a specific benchmark that each question is testing. The answer key that follows lists the benchmark for each question. Use the skills listed to identify skills that the student is lacking. Then target revision and instruction accordingly.

Practice Set 1

Question	Answer	Benchmark
1	C	MA.K.NSO.1.1 Given a group of up to 20 objects, count the number of objects in that group and represent the number of objects with a written numeral. State the number of objects in a rearrangement of that group without recounting.
2	D	MA.K.NSO.2.1 Recite the number names to 100 by ones and by tens. Starting at a given number, count forward within 100 and backward within 20.
3	C	MA.K.AR.1.1 For any number from 1 to 9, find the number that makes 10 when added to the given number.
4	B	MA.K.M.1.1 Identify the attributes of a single object that can be measured such as length, volume or weight.
5	D	MA.K.GR.1.1 Identify two- and three-dimensional figures regardless of their size or orientation. Figures are limited to circles, triangles, rectangles, squares, spheres, cubes, cones and cylinders.
6	C	MA.K.DP.1.1 Collect and sort objects into categories and compare the categories by counting the objects in each category. Report the results verbally, with a written numeral or with drawings.

Practice Set 2

Question	Answer	Benchmark
1	A	MA.K.NSO.1.2 Given a number from 0 to 20, count out that many objects.
2	A	MA.K.NSO.2.2 Represent whole numbers from 10 to 20, using a unit of ten and a group of ones, with objects, drawings and expressions or equations.
3	B	MA.K.AR.1.2 Given a number from 0 to 10, find the different ways it can be represented as the sum of two numbers.
4	C	MA.K.M.1.2 Directly compare two objects that have an attribute which can be measured in common. Express the comparison using language to describe the difference.
5	D	MA.K.GR.1.2 Compare two-dimensional figures based on their similarities, differences and positions. Sort two-dimensional figures based on their similarities and differences.
6	C	MA.K.DP.1.1 Collect and sort objects into categories and compare the categories by counting the objects in each category. Report the results verbally, with a written numeral or with drawings.

Practice Set 3

Question	Answer	Benchmark
1	B	MA.K.NSO.1.3 Identify positions of objects within a sequence using the words "first," "second," "third," "fourth" or "fifth."
2	B	MA.K.NSO.2.3 Locate, order and compare numbers from 0 to 20 using the number line and terms less than, equal to or greater than.
3	C	MA.K.AR.1.3 Solve addition and subtraction real-world problems using objects, drawings or equations to represent the problem.
4	C	MA.K.M.1.3 Express the length of an object, up to 20 units long, as a whole number of lengths by laying non-standard objects end to end with no gaps or overlaps.
5	D	MA.K.GR.1.3 Compare three-dimensional figures based on their similarities, differences and positions. Sort three-dimensional figures based on their similarities and differences.
6	A	MA.K.DP.1.1 Collect and sort objects into categories and compare the categories by counting the objects in each category. Report the results verbally, with a written numeral or with drawings.

Practice Set 4

Question	Answer	Benchmark
1	C	MA.K.NSO.1.4 Compare the number of objects from 0 to 20 in two groups using the terms less than, equal to or greater than.
2	D	MA.K.NSO.3.1 Explore addition of two whole numbers from 0 to 10, and related subtraction facts.
3	A	MA.K.AR.2.1 Explain why addition or subtraction equations are true using objects or drawings.
4	C	MA.K.M.1.1 Identify the attributes of a single object that can be measured such as length, volume or weight.
5	B	MA.K.GR.1.4 Find real-world objects that can be modeled by a given two- or three-dimensional figure. Figures are limited to circles, triangles, rectangles, squares, spheres, cubes, cones and cylinders.
6	C	MA.K.DP.1.1 Collect and sort objects into categories and compare the categories by counting the objects in each category. Report the results verbally, with a written numeral or with drawings.

Practice Set 5

Question	Answer	Benchmark
1	B	MA.K.NSO.1.1 Given a group of up to 20 objects, count the number of objects in that group and represent the number of objects with a written numeral. State the number of objects in a rearrangement of that group without recounting.
2	D	MA.K.NSO.3.2 Add two one-digit whole numbers with sums from 0 to 10 and subtract using related facts with procedural reliability.
3	C	MA.K.AR.1.1 For any number from 1 to 9, find the number that makes 10 when added to the given number.
4	B	MA.K.M.1.2 Directly compare two objects that have an attribute which can be measured in common. Express the comparison using language to describe the difference.
5	B	MA.K.GR.1.5 Combine two-dimensional figures to form a given composite figure. Figures used to form a composite shape are limited to triangles, rectangles and squares.
6	C	MA.K.DP.1.1 Collect and sort objects into categories and compare the categories by counting the objects in each category. Report the results verbally, with a written numeral or with drawings.

Practice Set 6

Question	Answer	Benchmark
1	B	MA.K.NSO.1.2 Given a number from 0 to 20, count out that many objects.
2	B	MA.K.NSO.2.1 Recite the number names to 100 by ones and by tens. Starting at a given number, count forward within 100 and backward within 20.
3	B	MA.K.AR.1.2 Given a number from 0 to 10, find the different ways it can be represented as the sum of two numbers.
4	C	MA.K.M.1.3 Express the length of an object, up to 20 units long, as a whole number of lengths by laying non-standard objects end to end with no gaps or overlaps.
5	B	MA.K.GR.1.1 Identify two- and three-dimensional figures regardless of their size or orientation. Figures are limited to circles, triangles, rectangles, squares, spheres, cubes, cones and cylinders.
6	A	MA.K.DP.1.1 Collect and sort objects into categories and compare the categories by counting the objects in each category. Report the results verbally, with a written numeral or with drawings.

Practice Set 7

Question	Answer	Benchmark
1	C	MA.K.NSO.1.3 Identify positions of objects within a sequence using the words "first," "second," "third," "fourth" or "fifth."
2	B	MA.K.NSO.2.2 Represent whole numbers from 10 to 20, using a unit of ten and a group of ones, with objects, drawings and expressions or equations.
3	C	MA.K.AR.1.3 Solve addition and subtraction real-world problems using objects, drawings or equations to represent the problem.
4	B	MA.K.M.1.1 Identify the attributes of a single object that can be measured such as length, volume or weight.
5	D	MA.K.GR.1.2 Compare two-dimensional figures based on their similarities, differences and positions. Sort two-dimensional figures based on their similarities and differences.
6	B	MA.K.DP.1.1 Collect and sort objects into categories and compare the categories by counting the objects in each category. Report the results verbally, with a written numeral or with drawings.

Practice Set 8

Question	Answer	Benchmark
1	A	MA.K.NSO.1.4 Compare the number of objects from 0 to 20 in two groups using the terms less than, equal to or greater than.
2	A	MA.K.NSO.2.3 Locate, order and compare numbers from 0 to 20 using the number line and terms less than, equal to or greater than.
3	A	MA.K.AR.2.1 Explain why addition or subtraction equations are true using objects or drawings.
4	A	MA.K.M.1.2 Directly compare two objects that have an attribute which can be measured in common. Express the comparison using language to describe the difference.
5	B	MA.K.GR.1.3 Compare three-dimensional figures based on their similarities, differences and positions. Sort three-dimensional figures based on their similarities and differences.
6	A	MA.K.DP.1.1 Collect and sort objects into categories and compare the categories by counting the objects in each category. Report the results verbally, with a written numeral or with drawings.

Practice Set 9

Question	Answer	Benchmark
1	B	MA.K.NSO.1.1 Given a group of up to 20 objects, count the number of objects in that group and represent the number of objects with a written numeral. State the number of objects in a rearrangement of that group without recounting.
2	B	MA.K.NSO.3.1 Explore addition of two whole numbers from 0 to 10, and related subtraction facts.
3	A	MA.K.AR.1.1 For any number from 1 to 9, find the number that makes 10 when added to the given number.
4	C	MA.K.M.1.3 Express the length of an object, up to 20 units long, as a whole number of lengths by laying non-standard objects end to end with no gaps or overlaps.
5	A	MA.K.GR.1.4 Find real-world objects that can be modeled by a given two- or three-dimensional figure. Figures are limited to circles, triangles, rectangles, squares, spheres, cubes, cones and cylinders.
6	B	MA.K.DP.1.1 Collect and sort objects into categories and compare the categories by counting the objects in each category. Report the results verbally, with a written numeral or with drawings.

Practice Set 10

Question	Answer	Benchmark
1	D	MA.K.NSO.1.3 Identify positions of objects within a sequence using the words "first," "second," "third," "fourth" or "fifth."
2	C	MA.K.NSO.3.2 Add two one-digit whole numbers with sums from 0 to 10 and subtract using related facts with procedural reliability.
3	B	MA.K.AR.1.3 Solve addition and subtraction real-world problems using objects, drawings or equations to represent the problem.
4	C	MA.K.M.1.1 Identify the attributes of a single object that can be measured such as length, volume or weight.
5	B	MA.K.GR.1.5 Combine two-dimensional figures to form a given composite figure. Figures used to form a composite shape are limited to triangles, rectangles and squares.
6	B	MA.K.DP.1.1 Collect and sort objects into categories and compare the categories by counting the objects in each category. Report the results verbally, with a written numeral or with drawings.

FAST Mathematics Skills Workbook, Daily Star Practice, Kindergarten

Practice Set 11

Question	Answer	Benchmark
1	C	MA.K.NSO.1.1 Given a group of up to 20 objects, count the number of objects in that group and represent the number of objects with a written numeral. State the number of objects in a rearrangement of that group without recounting.
2	C	MA.K.NSO.2.1 Recite the number names to 100 by ones and by tens. Starting at a given number, count forward within 100 and backward within 20.
3	B	MA.K.NSO.3.1 Explore addition of two whole numbers from 0 to 10, and related subtraction facts.
4	C	MA.K.AR.1.1 For any number from 1 to 9, find the number that makes 10 when added to the given number.
5	C	MA.K.AR.2.1 Explain why addition or subtraction equations are true using objects or drawings.
6	D	MA.K.M.1.1 Identify the attributes of a single object that can be measured such as length, volume or weight.
7	C	MA.K.M.1.3 Express the length of an object, up to 20 units long, as a whole number of lengths by laying non-standard objects end to end with no gaps or overlaps.
8	D	MA.K.GR.1.1 Identify two- and three-dimensional figures regardless of their size or orientation. Figures are limited to circles, triangles, rectangles, squares, spheres, cubes, cones and cylinders.
9	B	MA.K.GR.1.5 Combine two-dimensional figures to form a given composite figure. Figures used to form a composite shape are limited to triangles, rectangles and squares.
10	B	MA.K.DP.1.1 Collect and sort objects into categories and compare the categories by counting the objects in each category. Report the results verbally, with a written numeral or with drawings.

Practice Set 12

Question	Answer	Benchmark
1	D	MA.K.NSO.1.2 Given a number from 0 to 20, count out that many objects.
2	A	MA.K.NSO.2.2 Represent whole numbers from 10 to 20, using a unit of ten and a group of ones, with objects, drawings and expressions or equations.
3	C	MA.K.NSO.3.2 Add two one-digit whole numbers with sums from 0 to 10 and subtract using related facts with procedural reliability.
4	C	MA.K.AR.1.2 Given a number from 0 to 10, find the different ways it can be represented as the sum of two numbers.
5	A	MA.K.AR.2.1 Explain why addition or subtraction equations are true using objects or drawings.
6	C	MA.K.M.1.2 Directly compare two objects that have an attribute which can be measured in common. Express the comparison using language to describe the difference.
7	B	MA.K.M.1.3 Express the length of an object, up to 20 units long, as a whole number of lengths by laying non-standard objects end to end with no gaps or overlaps.
8	A	MA.K.GR.1.4 Find real-world objects that can be modeled by a given two- or three-dimensional figure. Figures are limited to circles, triangles, rectangles, squares, spheres, cubes, cones and cylinders.
9	D	MA.K.GR.1.2 Compare two-dimensional figures based on their similarities, differences and positions. Sort two-dimensional figures based on their similarities and differences.
10	A	MA.K.DP.1.1 Collect and sort objects into categories and compare the categories by counting the objects in each category. Report the results verbally, with a written numeral or with drawings.

Practice Set 13

Question	Answer	Benchmark
1	C	MA.K.NSO.1.3 Identify positions of objects within a sequence using the words "first," "second," "third," "fourth" or "fifth."
2	D	MA.K.NSO.2.3 Locate, order and compare numbers from 0 to 20 using the number line and terms less than, equal to or greater than.
3	C	MA.K.NSO.3.1 Explore addition of two whole numbers from 0 to 10, and related subtraction facts.
4	B	MA.K.AR.1.3 Solve addition and subtraction real-world problems using objects, drawings or equations to represent the problem.
5	D	MA.K.AR.2.1 Explain why addition or subtraction equations are true using objects or drawings.
6	C	MA.K.M.1.1 Identify the attributes of a single object that can be measured such as length, volume or weight.
7	C	MA.K.M.1.3 Express the length of an object, up to 20 units long, as a whole number of lengths by laying non-standard objects end to end with no gaps or overlaps.
8	C	MA.K.GR.1.1 Identify two- and three-dimensional figures regardless of their size or orientation. Figures are limited to circles, triangles, rectangles, squares, spheres, cubes, cones and cylinders.
9	B	MA.K.GR.1.3 Compare three-dimensional figures based on their similarities, differences and positions. Sort three-dimensional figures based on their similarities and differences.
10	B	MA.K.DP.1.1 Collect and sort objects into categories and compare the categories by counting the objects in each category. Report the results verbally, with a written numeral or with drawings.

Practice Set 14

Question	Answer	Benchmark
1	A	MA.K.NSO.1.4 Compare the number of objects from 0 to 20 in two groups using the terms less than, equal to or greater than.
2	A	MA.K.NSO.2.1 Recite the number names to 100 by ones and by tens. Starting at a given number, count forward within 100 and backward within 20.
3	B	MA.K.NSO.3.2 Add two one-digit whole numbers with sums from 0 to 10 and subtract using related facts with procedural reliability.
4	B	MA.K.AR.1.1 For any number from 1 to 9, find the number that makes 10 when added to the given number.
5	A	MA.K.AR.2.1 Explain why addition or subtraction equations are true using objects or drawings.
6	A	MA.K.M.1.2 Directly compare two objects that have an attribute which can be measured in common. Express the comparison using language to describe the difference.
7	B	MA.K.M.1.3 Express the length of an object, up to 20 units long, as a whole number of lengths by laying non-standard objects end to end with no gaps or overlaps.
8	C	MA.K.GR.1.4 Find real-world objects that can be modeled by a given two- or three-dimensional figure. Figures are limited to circles, triangles, rectangles, squares, spheres, cubes, cones and cylinders.
9	C	MA.K.GR.1.5 Combine two-dimensional figures to form a given composite figure. Figures used to form a composite shape are limited to triangles, rectangles and squares.
10	C	MA.K.DP.1.1 Collect and sort objects into categories and compare the categories by counting the objects in each category. Report the results verbally, with a written numeral or with drawings.

Practice Set 15

Question	Answer	Benchmark
1	D	MA.K.NSO.1.1 Given a group of up to 20 objects, count the number of objects in that group and represent the number of objects with a written numeral. State the number of objects in a rearrangement of that group without recounting.
2	B	MA.K.NSO.2.2 Represent whole numbers from 10 to 20, using a unit of ten and a group of ones, with objects, drawings and expressions or equations.
3	B	MA.K.NSO.3.1 Explore addition of two whole numbers from 0 to 10, and related subtraction facts.
4	B	MA.K.AR.1.2 Given a number from 0 to 10, find the different ways it can be represented as the sum of two numbers.
5	B	MA.K.AR.2.1 Explain why addition or subtraction equations are true using objects or drawings.
6	C	MA.K.M.1.1 Identify the attributes of a single object that can be measured such as length, volume or weight.
7	C	MA.K.M.1.3 Express the length of an object, up to 20 units long, as a whole number of lengths by laying non-standard objects end to end with no gaps or overlaps.
8	D	MA.K.GR.1.1 Identify two- and three-dimensional figures regardless of their size or orientation. Figures are limited to circles, triangles, rectangles, squares, spheres, cubes, cones and cylinders.
9	C	MA.K.GR.1.2 Compare two-dimensional figures based on their similarities, differences and positions. Sort two-dimensional figures based on their similarities and differences.
10	D	MA.K.DP.1.1 Collect and sort objects into categories and compare the categories by counting the objects in each category. Report the results verbally, with a written numeral or with drawings.

Practice Set 16

Question	Answer	Benchmark
1	B	MA.K.NSO.1.2 Given a number from 0 to 20, count out that many objects.
2	D	MA.K.NSO.2.3 Locate, order and compare numbers from 0 to 20 using the number line and terms less than, equal to or greater than.
3	C	MA.K.NSO.3.2 Add two one-digit whole numbers with sums from 0 to 10 and subtract using related facts with procedural reliability.
4	C	MA.K.AR.1.3 Solve addition and subtraction real-world problems using objects, drawings or equations to represent the problem.
5	C	MA.K.AR.2.1 Explain why addition or subtraction equations are true using objects or drawings.
6	B	MA.K.M.1.2 Directly compare two objects that have an attribute which can be measured in common. Express the comparison using language to describe the difference.
7	B	MA.K.M.1.3 Express the length of an object, up to 20 units long, as a whole number of lengths by laying non-standard objects end to end with no gaps or overlaps.
8	B	MA.K.GR.1.4 Find real-world objects that can be modeled by a given two- or three-dimensional figure. Figures are limited to circles, triangles, rectangles, squares, spheres, cubes, cones and cylinders.
9	B	MA.K.GR.1.3 Compare three-dimensional figures based on their similarities, differences and positions. Sort three-dimensional figures based on their similarities and differences.
10	B	MA.K.DP.1.1 Collect and sort objects into categories and compare the categories by counting the objects in each category. Report the results verbally, with a written numeral or with drawings.

FAST Mathematics Skills Workbook, Daily Star Practice, Kindergarten

Practice Set 17

Question	Answer	Benchmark
1	C	MA.K.NSO.1.3 Identify positions of objects within a sequence using the words "first," "second," "third," "fourth" or "fifth."
2	D	MA.K.NSO.2.1 Recite the number names to 100 by ones and by tens. Starting at a given number, count forward within 100 and backward within 20.
3	C	MA.K.NSO.3.1 Explore addition of two whole numbers from 0 to 10, and related subtraction facts.
4	B	MA.K.AR.1.1 For any number from 1 to 9, find the number that makes 10 when added to the given number.
5	A	MA.K.AR.2.1 Explain why addition or subtraction equations are true using objects or drawings.
6	A	MA.K.M.1.1 Identify the attributes of a single object that can be measured such as length, volume or weight.
7	B	MA.K.M.1.3 Express the length of an object, up to 20 units long, as a whole number of lengths by laying non-standard objects end to end with no gaps or overlaps.
8	C	MA.K.GR.1.1 Identify two- and three-dimensional figures regardless of their size or orientation. Figures are limited to circles, triangles, rectangles, squares, spheres, cubes, cones and cylinders.
9	C	MA.K.GR.1.5 Combine two-dimensional figures to form a given composite figure. Figures used to form a composite shape are limited to triangles, rectangles and squares.
10	C	MA.K.DP.1.1 Collect and sort objects into categories and compare the categories by counting the objects in each category. Report the results verbally, with a written numeral or with drawings.

Practice Set 18

Question	Answer	Benchmark
1	A	MA.K.NSO.1.4 Compare the number of objects from 0 to 20 in two groups using the terms less than, equal to or greater than.
2	A	MA.K.NSO.2.2 Represent whole numbers from 10 to 20, using a unit of ten and a group of ones, with objects, drawings and expressions or equations.
3	B	MA.K.NSO.3.2 Add two one-digit whole numbers with sums from 0 to 10 and subtract using related facts with procedural reliability.
4	C	MA.K.AR.1.2 Given a number from 0 to 10, find the different ways it can be represented as the sum of two numbers.
5	B	MA.K.AR.2.1 Explain why addition or subtraction equations are true using objects or drawings.
6	D	MA.K.M.1.2 Directly compare two objects that have an attribute which can be measured in common. Express the comparison using language to describe the difference.
7	B	MA.K.M.1.3 Express the length of an object, up to 20 units long, as a whole number of lengths by laying non-standard objects end to end with no gaps or overlaps.
8	D	MA.K.GR.1.4 Find real-world objects that can be modeled by a given two- or three-dimensional figure. Figures are limited to circles, triangles, rectangles, squares, spheres, cubes, cones and cylinders.
9	C	MA.K.GR.1.2 Compare two-dimensional figures based on their similarities, differences and positions. Sort two-dimensional figures based on their similarities and differences.
10	B	MA.K.DP.1.1 Collect and sort objects into categories and compare the categories by counting the objects in each category. Report the results verbally, with a written numeral or with drawings.

Practice Set 19

Question	Answer	Benchmark
1	C	MA.K.NSO.1.1 Given a group of up to 20 objects, count the number of objects in that group and represent the number of objects with a written numeral. State the number of objects in a rearrangement of that group without recounting.
2	B	MA.K.NSO.2.3 Locate, order and compare numbers from 0 to 20 using the number line and terms less than, equal to or greater than.
3	B	MA.K.NSO.3.1 Explore addition of two whole numbers from 0 to 10, and related subtraction facts.
4	C	MA.K.AR.1.3 Solve addition and subtraction real-world problems using objects, drawings or equations to represent the problem.
5	D	MA.K.AR.2.1 Explain why addition or subtraction equations are true using objects or drawings.
6	D	MA.K.M.1.1 Identify the attributes of a single object that can be measured such as length, volume or weight.
7	C	MA.K.M.1.3 Express the length of an object, up to 20 units long, as a whole number of lengths by laying non-standard objects end to end with no gaps or overlaps.
8	C	MA.K.GR.1.1 Identify two- and three-dimensional figures regardless of their size or orientation. Figures are limited to circles, triangles, rectangles, squares, spheres, cubes, cones and cylinders.
9	B	MA.K.GR.1.3 Compare three-dimensional figures based on their similarities, differences and positions. Sort three-dimensional figures based on their similarities and differences.
10	A	MA.K.DP.1.1 Collect and sort objects into categories and compare the categories by counting the objects in each category. Report the results verbally, with a written numeral or with drawings.

FAST Mathematics Skills Workbook, Daily Star Practice, Kindergarten

Practice Set 20

Question	Answer	Benchmark
1	A	MA.K.NSO.1.3 Identify positions of objects within a sequence using the words "first," "second," "third," "fourth" or "fifth."
2	B	MA.K.NSO.2.1 Recite the number names to 100 by ones and by tens. Starting at a given number, count forward within 100 and backward within 20.
3	C	MA.K.NSO.3.2 Add two one-digit whole numbers with sums from 0 to 10 and subtract using related facts with procedural reliability.
4	C	MA.K.AR.1.1 For any number from 1 to 9, find the number that makes 10 when added to the given number.
5	C	MA.K.AR.2.1 Explain why addition or subtraction equations are true using objects or drawings.
6	A	MA.K.M.1.2 Directly compare two objects that have an attribute which can be measured in common. Express the comparison using language to describe the difference.
7	C	MA.K.M.1.3 Express the length of an object, up to 20 units long, as a whole number of lengths by laying non-standard objects end to end with no gaps or overlaps.
8	A	MA.K.GR.1.4 Find real-world objects that can be modeled by a given two- or three-dimensional figure. Figures are limited to circles, triangles, rectangles, squares, spheres, cubes, cones and cylinders.
9	A	MA.K.GR.1.5 Combine two-dimensional figures to form a given composite figure. Figures used to form a composite shape are limited to triangles, rectangles and squares.
10	D	MA.K.DP.1.1 Collect and sort objects into categories and compare the categories by counting the objects in each category. Report the results verbally, with a written numeral or with drawings.